UNIFORMS
OF THE
UNITED STATES ARMY
1774–1889
in Full Color

H. A. Ogden

DOVER PUBLICATIONS, INC.
Mineola, New York

Copyright

Copyright © 1998 by Dover Publications, Inc.
All rights reserved under Pan American and International Copyright Conventions.

Published in Canada by General Publishing Company, Ltd., 30 Lesmill Road, Don Mills, Toronto, Ontario.
Published in the United Kingdom by Constable and Company, Ltd., 3 The Lanchesters, 162–164 Fulham Palace Road, London W6 9ER.

Bibliographical Note

Uniforms of the United States Army, 1774–1889, in Full Color, first published by Dover Publications, Inc., in 1998, is a partial republication of the work published in 1890 by the Quartermaster General of the Army of the United States as *Uniform of the Army of the United States, Illustrated, From 1774 to 1889.* The Dover edition includes the 44 full-color plates, the title of each plate, and captions adapted from the Key to Illustrations in the original work.

Library of Congress Cataloging-in-Publication Data

Ogden, Henry Alexander, 1856–1936.
    Uniforms of the United States Army, 1774–1889, in full color / H. A. Ogden.
        p.   cm.
    Originally published: Uniform of the Army of the United States, illustrated, from 1774 to 1889. Washington, D. C. : Quartermaster General of the Army of the United States, 1890.
    ISBN 0-486-40107-3 (pbk.)
    1. United States. Army–Uniforms–History–18th century. 2. United States. Army–Uniforms–History–19th century. I. Ogden, Henry Alexander, 1856–1936. Uniform of the Army of the United States, illustrated, from 1774 to 1889. II. Title.
UG483.036   1998
355.1'4'097309034–dc21   97-46753
                                                                              CIP

Manufactured in the United States of America
Dover Publications, Inc., 31 East 2nd Street, Mineola, N.Y. 11501

Introduction

In 1890, the Army of the United States published a volume including all regulations that had been issued since the formation of the Continental Army in 1775 (and some related to the Minute Men of Massachusetts), pertaining to official uniform. The book, entitled *Uniform of the Army of the United States, Illustrated, From 1774 to 1889,* featured 44 full-color plates of paintings by artist H. A. Ogden.

In carrying out his commission, Ogden composed a wide variety of scenes in which were featured officers and enlisted men from many different Army services, in diverse settings and activities. To show the various uniforms where and when they would be worn in actual military circumstances, he portrayed natural-looking groupings and interactions, such as soldiers reading their mail or playing checkers in garrison; officers conferring or reporting in urban townhouses or rural mansions; the activity of a campaign encampment; soldiers marching or carrying messages in open country; or cadets and officers at the U.S. Military Academy at West Point, N.Y. Ogden included portraits of several well-known generals, and even painted specific officers of lesser rank who were his contemporaries.

This Dover publication, *Uniforms of the United States Army, 1774-1889, in Full Color,* reproduces all 44 of Ogden's detailed paintings, with captions identifying the Army service and rank of each soldier whose uniform is presented. From the infantry and sharpshooters of the Revolutionary War to the cavalry who fought the last of the Indian Wars, and from full-dress uniform to campaign garb to fatigues, a wide range of U.S. Army uniforms is featured in this unique collection of full-color plates.

List of Plates

Plate 1. Independent Company Organizations, 1774–1775.

Shown, from left to right, are the uniforms of the Virginia Infantry; a Minute Man or Militiaman; the First Company, Governor's Foot Guard of Connecticut; the First City Troop of Philadelphia; and a Minute Man.

Plate 2. Miscellaneous Organizations, Continental Army, 1776–1779.

Shown, from left to right, are the uniforms of the Third Pennsylvania Regiment; Washington's Guard; Second Regiment, South Carolina Infantry; Eleventh Virginia Regiment (also worn by the soldier in the distance); and Maryland Riflemen.

Plate 3. Commander-in-Chief, Aide-de-Camp, Line Officers, etc., 1779–1783.

Shown, from left to right, are the uniforms of an aide-de-camp to the commander-in-chief, a private of Moylan's Dragoons, the commander-in-chief (George Washington), a lieutenant of infantry, and a captain of artillery.

Plate 4. Infantry: Continental Army, 1779–1783.

Four different uniforms, in accordance with their home area, were worn by these infantrymen from the thirteen colonies; at left in the group in the foreground is seen the uniform worn by lieutenants of infantry from New Hampshire, Massachusetts, Rhode Island, and Connecticut.

Plate 5. Artillery, 1777–1783.

Shown are the uniforms of an enlisted man in the artillery (at left, behind cannon), a field officer of artillery (on horseback), a company officer of artillery (saluting), and four enlisted men in the artillery (to the right of the others).

Plate 6. Light Infantry, 1782.

Uniforms depicted are of a dragoon of "Lee's Legion" (left, on horseback); a major-general, France's Marquis de Lafayette (center, on horseback), when commanding light infantry; and privates of light infantry (background and right).

Plate 7. Infantry and Artillery, 1783–1796.

The uniforms of enlisted men in the infantry (at left, in background) and a captain of infantry (at left, in foreground) are seen along with those of a captain of artillery (at right, in foreground) and enlisted men in the artillery (at right, in far background).

Plate 8. Infantry and Musicians, 1796–1799.

The uniforms of privates in the infantry (in a row, at left), a company officer of infantry (in foreground), and musicians (at right, in background) are shown.

Plate 9. Cavalry, Infantry, Artillery, 1799–1802.

Seen here are the uniforms of an enlisted man in the infantry (at left, near tent), an enlisted man in the cavalry (holding the horse's reins), a lieutenant of infantry (right of center), and a lieutenant of artillery (at right).

Plate 10. Commander-in-Chief and Staff, 1799–1802.

From left to right, the uniforms of the Quartermaster-General, a brigadier-general, a major-general, the commander-in-chief, and the inspector-general are shown.

Plate 11. Infantry and Artillery, 1802–1810.

From left to right, the uniforms of a private in the artillery, a private in the infantry, a captain of artillery, and a captain of infantry are shown.

Plate 12. General, Staff, and Infantry, 1810–1813.

The uniform of a captain of infantry (at left, with back to troops) is seen with those of enlisted men in the infantry (first row of assembled troops), and, on horseback, a major-general, a brigadier-general, an aide-de-camp, and a colonel of infantry.

Plate 13. Artillery, Infantry, Rifle, Dragoon, Cadet, 1813–1821.

In this scene are depicted a cadet at the U.S. Military Academy at West Point (at left in background) with a lieutenant of artillery; privates in the infantry, rifles, and artillery (left to right, in foreground); a sergeant in the light artillery (on horseback, in background at right); and a sergeant in the light dragoons (standing next to him).

Plate 14. General, Staff and Line Officers, Light Artillery, 1813–1821.

Shown here are the uniforms of a colonel of infantry (on horseback) and, from left to right, a captain of light infantry, the quartermaster-general, a colonel of artillery, a major-general (Andrew Jackson, who commanded at the Battle of New Orleans during the War of 1812), and the Adjutant and Inspector-General.

Plate 15. Regimental Officers, Engineer, and Cadet, 1821–1832.

Here, from left to right, are seen the uniforms of a colonel of artillery, a major of engineers, a captain of infantry, a captain of artillery, and a cadet in the U.S. Military Academy at West Point (uniform worn 1816-1821).

Plate 16. Major-General, Staff and Line Officers, Cadets, 1832–1835.

Illustrated here is the uniform of cadets in the U.S. Military Academy (at left, in background), along with: (from left to right in foreground group) the uniforms of a colonel of artillery, a major-general, a field officer of infantry, an officer of the Quartermaster's Department, an officer of the Subsistence Department, and an aide-de-camp to the major-general; and (at right, in the background) an officer of the Ordnance Corps, an instructor at the Academy, and a medical officer.

Plate 17. Enlisted Men: Artillery, Infantry, Dragoons (Full Dress), 1835–1850.

Shown here are the uniforms of privates in the infantry (one standing at left, another standing in center background), a private in the artillery (standing at left, with service chevron on sleeve), an artillery sergeant (seated), a musician (private of infantry), a corporal in the infantry, and a sergeant in the dragoons (on horseback, in background).

Plate 18. Major-General, Staff and Line Officers (Undress), 1841–1850.

The uniforms depicted are those of a private in the dragoons (at left, with horse, in background), a colonel of artillery, a staff captain, a major of ordnance, a lieutenant-colonel of engineers, a major-general (Zachary Taylor), and (in background, at right) a colonel of infantry, on horseback, and a captain of artillery.

Plate 19. Voltigeur, Infantry, Dragoon, Artillery (Campaign Uniform), 1841–1851.

Shown here are the uniforms of a private voltigeur (a foot rifleman), a corporal in the infantry (seated), a private in the infantry, a corporal in the dragoons (on horseback), and privates in the artillery (in background, right, with horse team and gun carriage).

Plate 20. Major-General, Staff and Line Officers, 1851–1858.

The uniforms seen are of (the first five officers on horseback, from the left): an officer in the Quartermaster's Department, a major-general, an officer in the Inspector-General's Department, an officer in the Adjutant-General's Department, and an officer in the Pay Department; also (standing in the foreground), a captain of infantry, (next on horseback) an officer in the Subsistence Department, (in the middle of the trio on foot) an officer in the Medical Department, (last on horseback) an aide-de-camp, and standing (right foreground) a lieutenant of foot rifles and (right background) a private of infantry.

Plate 21. Engineers, Foot Rifles, Dragoons (Musician), Light Artillery, Infantry, 1851–1854.

The uniforms in this scene are those of a private in the infantry (at left, with rifle), a musician in the infantry (at left in group near archway in background), musicians in the artillery (to the right of him), a quartermaster sergeant in the engineers (standing at left in group in foreground), a private in the rifles (seated at left, playing checkers), a musician in the dragoons (standing in center), a private in the light artillery (watching checker game), and a first sergeant in the infantry (at right, playing checkers).

Plate 22. Artillery, Ordnance, and Engineers, 1851–1858.

From left to right, the uniforms shown are those of a first sergeant in the artillery, a colonel of artillery, a first lieutenant of artillery (regimental quartermaster), a second lieutenant of engineers, a major of ordnance, and an ordnance sergeant.

Plate 23. Cavalry and Dragoons, 1855–1858.

Shown in this scene, from left to right, are the uniforms of a private in the cavalry, a captain of cavalry, a major of dragoons, a private in the dragoons, and a first sergeant in the dragoons.

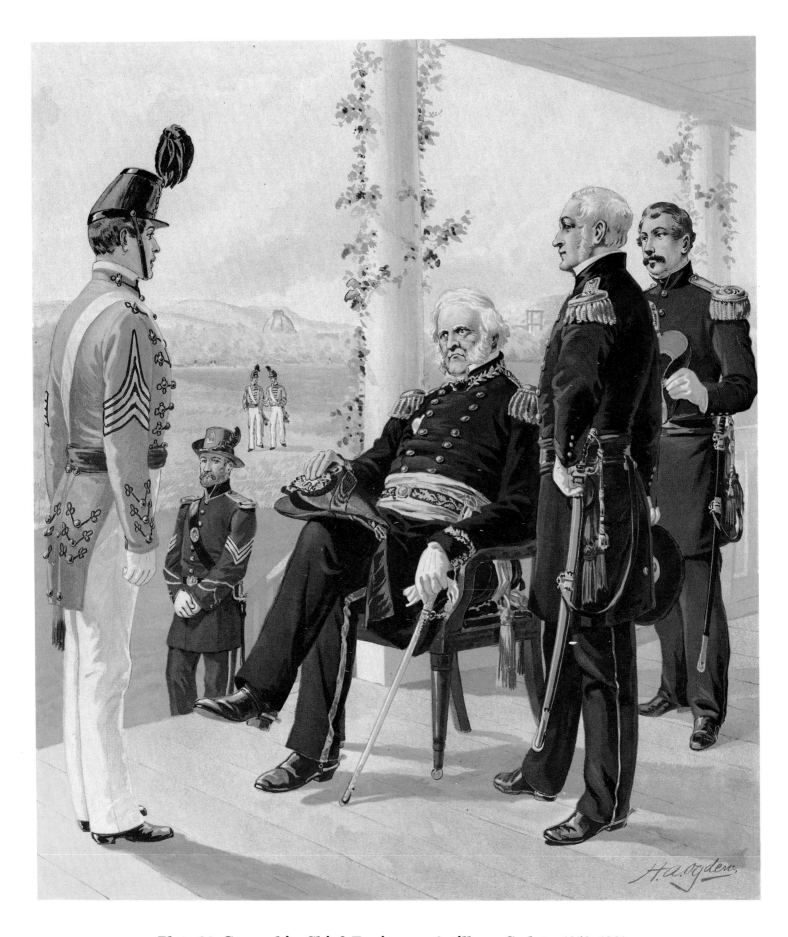

Plate 24. General-in-Chief, Engineers, Artillery, Cadets, 1858–1861.

The uniforms seen in the foreground are those of a captain of cadets (at left), a sergeant of engineers, a general-in-chief (Winfield Scott), a colonel of engineers, and a first lieutenant of artillery.

Plate 25. Artillery, Infantry, Mounted Rifles, Light Artillery, 1858–1861.

Seen in full dress uniform are (at left, in the background) a private and a field officer in the artillery; (at left, in the foreground) another private in the artillery, with a first sergeant in the infantry; and (seated, in the background) a corporal in the mounted rifles, with (standing) a private in the light artillery.

Plate 26. Staff, Field, and Line Officers and Enlisted Men, 1858–1861.

Shown are the uniforms of (inside the building entrance) a field officer of the general staff and a lieutenant of cavalry; (from left to right, in the foreground) a lieutenant-colonel of mounted rifles, a major of dragoons, and a captain of infantry; and (at right) a private in the infantry (with shouldered rifle) and a sergeant in the dragoons.

Plate 27. Campaign Uniform: Field, Line, and Noncommissioned Officers and Privates, 1861–1866.

This scene shows the campaign uniforms of (on the white horse) a sergeant in the light artillery, (on the chestnut horse) a lieutenant-colonel of artillery, (speaking with him) a first lieutenant of infantry, (leading the company) a corporal in the infantry, and (behind him and to his right) privates in the infantry.

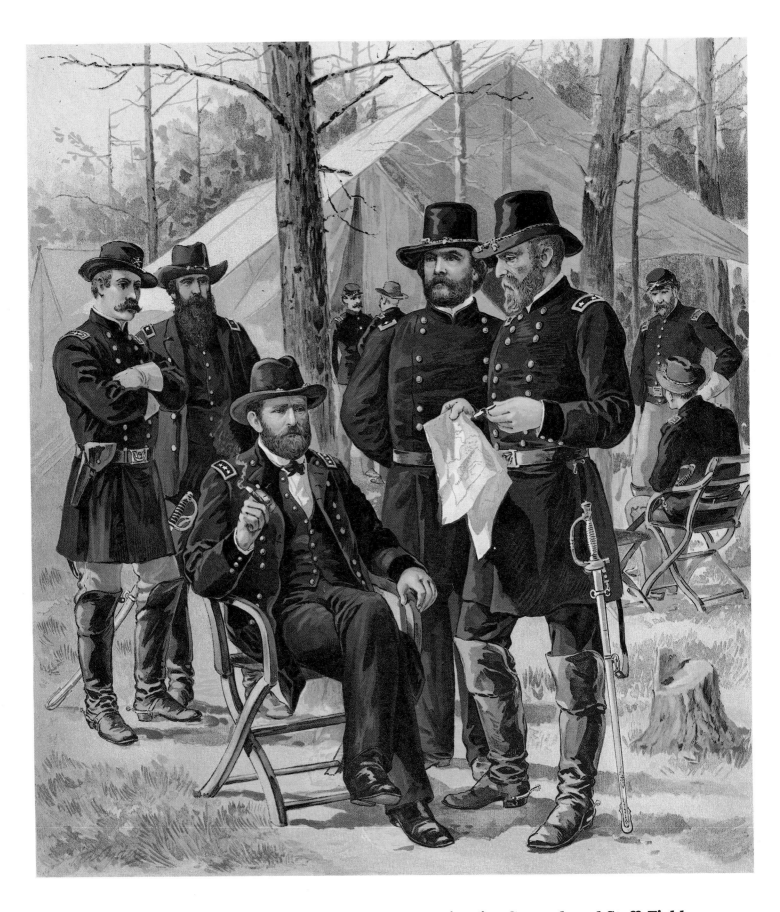

Plate 28. Lieutenant-General, Major-General, Brigadier-General, and Staff, Field, and Line Officers, 1861–1866.

The uniforms seen (from left to right) are those of a colonel of cavalry, a brigadier-general, and (seated) a lieutenant-general–U. S. Grant; (in the background) two infantry officers; a brigadier-general and a major-general (George Meade, holding map); and (at right, in background) an officer of artillery and an officer of infantry.

Plate 29. Major-General, Staff and Line Officers, and Enlisted Men (Full Dress), 1862–1871.

These uniforms were worn by an enlisted man in the infantry (outdoors, at left), an enlisted man in the light artillery, and (from left to right, indoors) a field officer of cavalry, a captain of artillery, an officer of infantry, an officer of light artillery (with red plume), a private in the artillery, a major-general, an officer in the Medical Department, and the captain of the general staff.

Plate 30. Officers and Enlisted Men: Cavalry, Artillery, Infantry (Full Dress), 1872–1881.

Seen from left to right are the uniforms of a private in the light artillery (in the background), a captain of light artillery and a company officer of artillery (standing), a field officer of cavalry and a field officer of infantry (on horseback), a sergeant in the cavalry, a corporal in the infantry, and a private in the artillery.

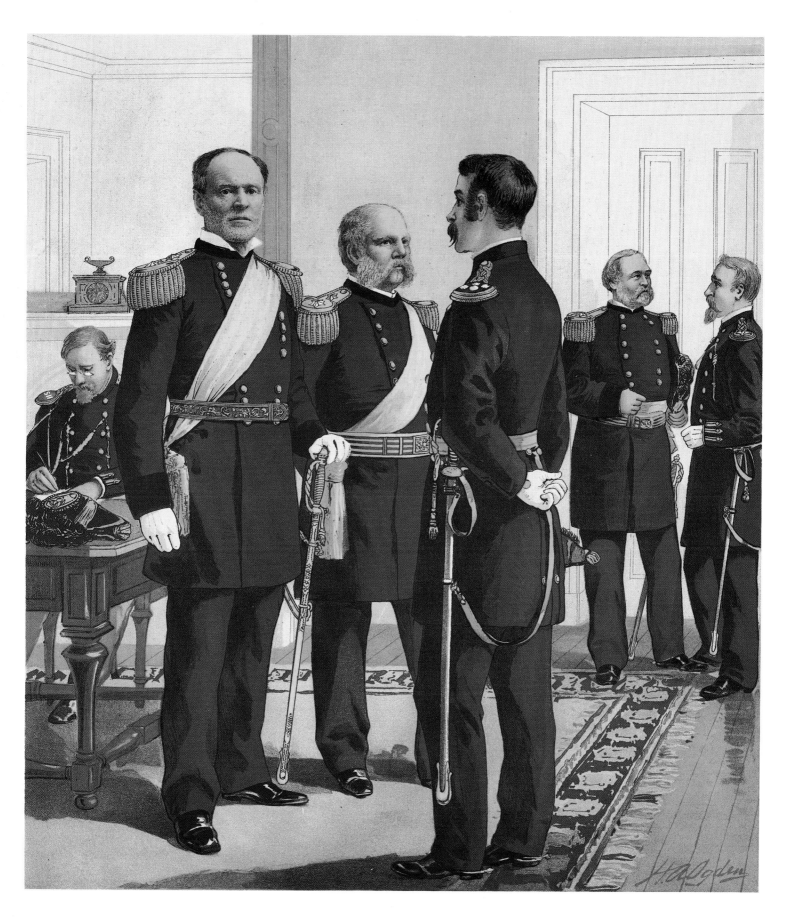

Plate 31. General, Major-General, and Officers of General Staff, 1872–1880.

From left to right are depicted the uniforms of a captain of artillery (seated) who is an aide-de-camp to the major-general, a general (William T. Sherman is portrayed), a major-general, a lieutenant-colonel of ordnance, a brigadier-general of the general staff, and a colonel who is an aide-de-camp to the general.

Plate 32. Field and Line Officers, Heavy Artillery and Infantry, and Enlisted Men, 1880–1885.

In this scene are illustrated the uniforms of (far background) a private in the infantry, (middle ground) a corporal in the artillery and a private in the infantry, and (foreground, standing) a captain of artillery and a lieutenant of infantry, with (seated) a colonel of infantry.

Plate 33. Lieutenant-General, Staff and Line Officers (Full Dress), 1888.

Seen here, from left to right, are the uniforms of a lieutenant-general (Philip Sheridan is shown), a cavalry officer, a lieutenant-colonel in the general staff corps, an officer of the light artillery, and the Assistant Adjutant-General.

Plate 34. Major-General, Staff and Line Officers (Full Dress), 1888.

Depicted are a field officer of infantry (on the white horse), an officer of the general staff, a major-general (on the chestnut horse), a company officer of infantry, and a company officer of artillery.

Plate 35. Brigadier-General, Staff and Line Officers (Full Dress), 1888.

Shown here from left to right are the uniforms of a captain of cavalry, a brigadier-general (George Crook, in this case), a regimental adjutant of infantry, an officer of the general staff or staff corps, a regimental adjutant of artillery, and an officer of cavalry.

Plate 36. Officers, General Staff and Staff Corps (Full Dress), 1888.

Represented in this group are the uniforms of (standing) a colonel who is Assistant Adjutant-General, with a brigadier-general of the general staff and staff corps; and (seated) a brigadier-general who is Adjutant-General, a colonel in the engineer corps, and a brigadier-general who is Inspector-General.

Plate 37. Brigadier-General, Line Officers, Enlisted Men (Campaign Dress), 1888.

In this view are seen the uniforms of (standing) a company officer of light artillery, a field officer of infantry, a brigadier-general (Nelson A. Miles is portrayed), a company officer of cavalry, and (at right, on horseback) enlisted men in the cavalry.

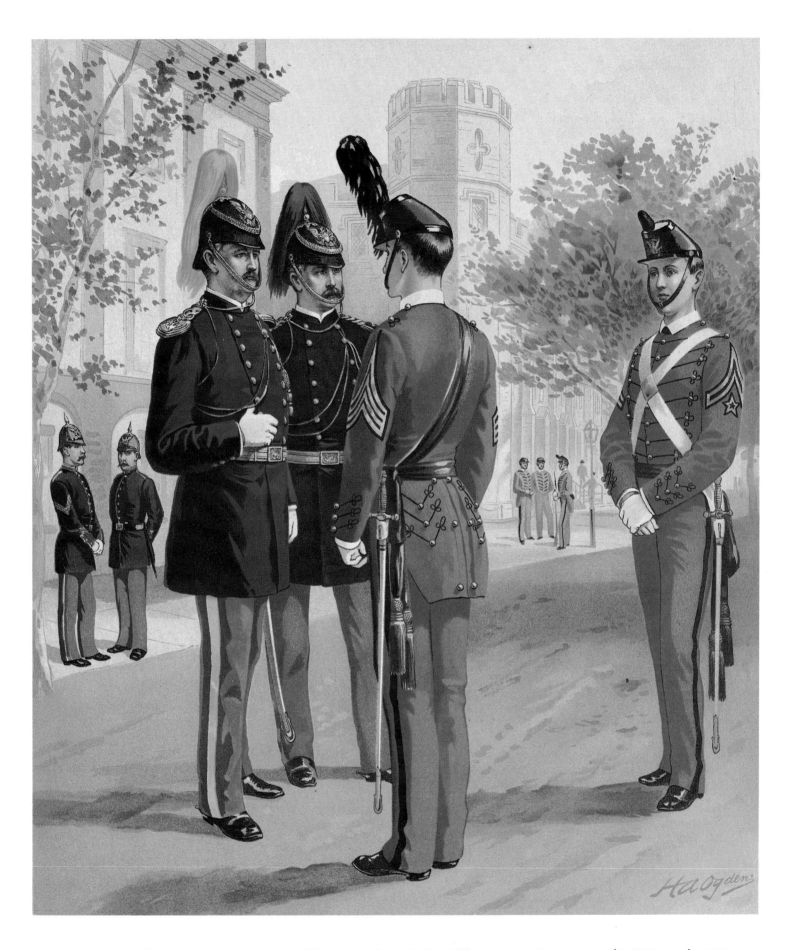

Plate 38. Officers, Cavalry and Artillery; Cadets, U.S. Military Academy; etc. (Full Dress), 1888.

Visible at left, in the background, are the uniforms of a sergeant and a private in the engineers; in the foreground are seen those of a field officer of cavalry, a field officer of artillery, and a cadet captain at the U.S. Military Academy; in the far background, three cadets at the U.S. Military Academy are seen (two in full dress uniform and one in undress); at right is a cadet color sergeant, U.S. Military Academy.

Plate 39. Staff and Line Officers (Full Dress), Chaplain, etc., 1888.

Seen from left to right are the uniforms of an officer in the signal corps, an officer of the general staff corps, a chaplain, an officer in the Inspector-General's Department, a field officer of infantry, a company officer of infantry (in undress uniform, with cork helmet), and a company officer of infantry in full dress uniform.

Plate 40. Officers and Enlisted Men (Overcoats and Capes), 1888.

Seen in the background, at left, are the uniforms of two officers with capes; in the foreground are seen the uniforms of a general officer, a lieutenant-colonel of artillery, a captain of cavalry, and a corporal of cavalry.

Plate 41. Noncommissioned Officers, Staff Corps, etc. (Full Dress), 1888.

Shown here are the uniforms of a sergeant in the signal corps (walking) and a musician in the artillery, an ordnance sergeant, a post commissary sergeant, a post quartermaster sergeant (seated), and a hospital steward.

Plate 42. Enlisted Men, Staff Corps and Artillery (Full Dress), 1888.

In this scene are shown, from left to right, the uniforms of a private in the light artillery, a private in the artillery, a musician in the light artillery, a private in the signal corps, a sergeant-major in the artillery, a first sergeant in the light artillery, and an ordnance sergeant.

Plate 43. Enlisted Men, Cavalry and Infantry (Full Dress), 1888.

The uniform of a trumpeter in the cavalry is seen at the far left; in the foreground are seen the uniforms of a corporal in the infantry, a private in the cavalry (on horseback), and a sergeant in the cavalry; at right are shown a private in the infantry and a musician in the infantry.

Plate 44. Enlisted Men (General Wear, Fatigue, etc.), 1888.

Depicted are an enlisted man wearing a fatigue hat and a canvas fatigue suit; a cavalryman with a fatigue hat, stable frock, and overalls; a quartermaster sergeant in the infantry, with a summer helmet and dress for general wear; a saddler sergeant of cavalry, wearing a forage cap and dress for general wear; and a private in the cavalry (on horseback), wearing a forage cap and dress for general wear.